Silvia Comoglio

VIA CRUCIS

Translated by Giorgio Mobili

Fomite
Burlington, VT

ISBN-13: 978-1-959984-77-1
Library of Congress Control Number: 2024942811

Fomite
58 Peru Street
Burlington, VT 05401
www.fomitepress.com

10/09/2024

VIA CRUCIS

Maria Sua Madre come bimbo cullava questa vita
sparsa come perla fulgida e leggera all'ingresso
di un mondo che si filtra dentro la sua eco : férmo —
refolo che spoglia dell'alba la distanza, l'abisso —
natante di rugiada, esploso in terra sempiterna —

His Mother Mary cradled this life as she would a child
a life strewn as a light, radiant pearl at the entrance
of a world that seeps into its echo: a still —
gust that strips dawn of all distance, the abyss —
a vessel made from dew, burst into sempiternal earth —

Prima Stazione - Gesù è condannato a morte

Sfatto ora è il plenilunio in questa sola storia
di dubbio già molato nell'acqua di un bacile, sfatto —
a pura notte dove troppo vasto è il dire degli ottusi, il —
crocifiggi! ampliato e ripetuto in alberi ghermiti
da futili linguaggi : ombre immedicate, di taglio sulla porta,
tutte declinate in *chi dite che io sia* su echi sovrapposto
privati di ogni loro forma : immoto soffio che si inarca
a terra rovesciando ciottoli silenti di albe —
appena simulate cóntro cubiti di olmi e bocche —
e *pellicani!* tutti sparpagliati in lunga e minuziosa
mássima carezza —

———————————

First Station - Jesus Is Condemned to Death

The full moon has fully melted into this one story
of doubt already smoothed down by a basin's water, dissolved —
into total night, where too vast is the speech of the obtuse, that —
crucify! amplified and repeated by trees in thrall
to futile languages: unmedicated shadows, cast sideways on doors,
all of them uttered in that *who do you think I am* overlapping
now-shapeless echoes: a dull gust arching up only to topple
to the ground the silent cobblestones of barely simulated —
dawns looming up against cubits of elm trees, mouths —
and pelicans! all scattered in a long, meticulous
utmost caress —

———————————

SECONDA STAZIONE - GESÙ È CARICATO DELLA CROCE

Tu lo stesso, dolore impronunciato,
sei spargere sottile di un ordine del mondo
dove la forza che vigila nel Sempre, come se già fosse —
eco che si apre a duna della luce, fece di una spalla,
modesta di portata, soglia illimitata per un corpo
dívenuto dono di ogni sua larghezza là dove —
tutto si confonde tra il suono e il suo silenzio,
nell'albero che crebbe disperso e capovolto
in essenza pura di radice : cárdine che giunse —
déntro questo specchio dove è stabile guardare
stringere le dita all'ultima dimora, e crescere d'intero
il tempo deformato in lume del suo pianto : l'órma —
piantata qui di fronte, a báttito che smuove
fasci di radice dal bosco straripati, e —
nel tutto cá-mminati —

———————————

Second Station – Jesus Takes Up His Cross

Notwithstanding, you, unspeakable sorrow,
are the subtle spreading of a world order
wherein the force alert in the Always, as if it were —
an echo opening into a dune of light, turned a shoulder
but modest in size, into the limitless threshold for a body
which made every inch of its breadth into a gift, in the place —
where all is muddled between sound and silence,
in the tree that grew jumbled and upturned
in the pure essence of its roots: the hinge that reached —
into this mirror where we can stably watch this man
grasp the wood of his ultimate abode, watch time
fully expand, deformed into the light of his tears: his footprint —
dug here in front of us, as a heartbeat that shakes up
the clumps of roots that have overrun the woods and —
that we walk through in the whole —

———————————

Terza Stazione - Gesù cade sotto la croce

L' álbero che ha specchio dentro la sua foglia
è limite del viso che a lamina sottile allunga e poi biforca
taciti disgiunti lumi di paura nel Sempre
sempre coniugati in precise case alla deriva, *prismi* —
in cui cadere è ancora custodire l'abisso e la sua luce,
fermando, a punto certo di frontiera, la notte che si schiocca
pura negli sterpi di pagine girate nel modo —
più casuale : è devoto sospendere il discorso
di un tempo che fluisce, mutando in puro approdo
quest'óbolo di spazio in cui l'ombra è già recisa, e la fine —
fiorisce di eterno mio principio, se è pensato,
pensato all'infinito, il ventre, che alto di respiro,
cruna dopo cruna, esplode, déntro la sua luce, come —
amore e filo —

———————————

Third Station – Jesus Falls Under the Cross

The tree mirroring itself in its leaf is the edge
of the face that lengthens into a thin lamina, then splits
silent, loose glows of fear, in the Always
always embodied in distinct houses adrift, *prisms* —
where falling is still preserving the abyss and its light,
stopping, like a set frontier point, the total night that cracks
in the brushwood of pages turned in the most —
casual way: it is pious to suspend the discourse
of flowing time, changing this puny offering of space
of severed shadows into a pure haven, so that the end —
can bloom into my eternal beginning, when this
high-breathed womb is *thought through ad infinitum,*
a womb which, in passing through needles' eyes, explodes
inside its own light, like love and thread —

———————

Quarta Stazione - Gesù incontra sua madre

Vedi? questi occhi che vanno camminando
sono terre già fissate óltre il tempo
e sopra l'acqua, ore —
tenute sempre aperte per l'albero più alto
del giorno e dello spazio. Sono mondo —
in cui l'estremo *non posso più capire*
lo annulla il tuo sapermi soglia óltre —
questa soglia, luce che distende
l'antro di montagna, cesellando
lo spargersi del mondo in stupendo —
amore delirante, lingua che sola muta —
l'ombra che qui sembra tutta già compiuta
in dimora di vasto cielo aperto,
da guardare in silenzio e —
só-rridendo —

_____

Fourth Station – Jesus Meets His Mother

Can you see? These walking eyes
are lands already settled beyond time
and above water, hours —
kept forever open for the tallest tree of the day
and of space. They are world —
in which the ultimate *I cannot understand anymore*
is voided by your knowledge that I am threshold beyond —
this threshold, light unfolding
the mountain cave, chiseling
the spreading of the world into marvelous —
crazy love, the only language that can transform —
the shadow here — it seems — already fully resolved
in this dwelling of vast open skies,
to be watched in silence and —
with a smile —

————————————

Quinta Stazione - Gesù è aiutato dal Cireneo

Tu fosti questa terra che guarda di sorpresa
il buio da me scritto per leggere e capire —
un giorno vissuto ripetendo lingue a sua memoria,
e nato, nato ritrovato, perché ha pesi, *pesi immensi,*
per fissare questa vita all'orígine del mondo, pesi —
divisi a pieno in questo solo punto límpido di sazi
últimi crinali, di un téndere sull'acqua di álberi e paesi
feroci e circolari, *bócche* di unica parola —
che guarda senza fiato quanto sembrerebbe
radice di follia ma è sguardo ampliato da sua eco,
ora che fiorisce, in lunga trasparenza, tra i contorti
rami della sera : *case* di etere e silenzio —
del tutto spalancate di lucenti essenze inconosciute
nel bacio qui rimasto sempre ripetuto in lungo solo volo
líquido di specchio, Tempo che si apre di tútto —
il suo respiro —

———————

Fifth Station – Simon of Cyrene Helps Jesus Carry the Cross

You became this earth that gazes in astonishment
upon the darkness I have written to be read and understood —
a day which we live by repeating tongues in its memory,
a day that is born, born having found itself, because it has weights,
immense weights, to fix this life at the origin of the world, weights
fully shared in this sole, pristine point of terminal
pain-sated ridges, of these trees and cruel circular villages
stretching over water, *mouths* for the only word —
that breathlessly gazes upon what would seem
the root of madness, yet is a gaze enhanced by its own echo,
an hour that blooms, long and transparent, amid the evening's
gnarled boughs: wide open *houses* of ether and silence —
giving forth their unknown essences
in the kiss left behind and always repeated
in one long liquid mirror flight, Time that opens up proffering —
all its breath —

――――――――――

Sesta Stazione - La Veronica asciuga il volto a Gesù

Nómini chi sono, tra gli orti e questa casa,
in un tempo a parola già prescelta, chi prese
un ramo del mio volto. Nómini e descriva
se essenza, sono, immota della fonte,
o enigma restato nella traccia di un sacro —
stupore delle labbra. Nómini e ripeta —
l'ocra che ricopre la cima di montagna,
e l'álbero e la nube, e quésta stessa terra,
e il tempo di sopra queste teste che è bagliore,
bagliore necessario, di un cantico sospeso
nell'estasi di istanti prossimi di soglia, di —
írrompere di mondi del tutto trasparenti,
a máttutino colpo dívampato in cielo —
bianco, a mar-gherita —

—————————

Sixth Station – Veronica Wipes the Face of Jesus

Let her name who I am, amid the gardens and this house,
in a time that is already-chosen word, she who took
a branch of my face. Let her name and describe
if I am the source's motionless essence,
or the enigma caught in the imprint of a sacred —
amazement of the lips. Let them name and repeat —
the ochre covering the mountaintop,
the tree and the cloud, and this very earth,
and the time above these heads which is light,
necessary light, of a song suspended
in the extasy of instants nearing the threshold, of —
the onslaught of thoroughly transparent worlds,
a morning blast flaring up in the sky —
white, daisy-like —

––––––––––––

Settima Stazione - Gesù cade per la seconda volta

Diáfano nell'aria l'atomo che passa
sempre parallelo al mondo già coniato,
ipotesi di viso cosciente e più vicino,
eco già confusa col bianco delle mura,
e moto che si accalca nel fiore alla radice,
nel punto in cui amare sgretola di nudo
il limite che viene di tempo a cominciare,
rovescio di fessura del rovo della terra
dove, a gemito che sono, il ventre si rimbalza
sempre più lontano, ríschiarando a luce
quanto qui si tace in ogni nostro pianto
inérpicato in gola in altezze miniate di —
crepaccio —

———————————

Seventh Station – Jesus Falls the Second Time

Diaphanous in the air is the atom that flies
always parallel to the already-coined world,
hypothesis of a conscious and closer face,
echo already blurred into the walls' whiteness,
and motion gathering at the root of the flower,
at the point in which the act of loving crushes and strips bare
the borderline that comes as time's beginning,
as the cleft's underside from the earth's brambles
where, reduced to a groan, the womb bounces
farther and farther, shedding light
over the thing we conceal in our weeping
which clambers up our throat to a crevasse's —
illuminated heights —

———————————

Ottava Stazione - Gesù consola le donne di Gerusalemme

Un astro in erranza dentro il suo prodigio
plasma e dopo solca i cedri e la cicogna,
e il cuore, il cuore vostro, sceso ad ali tarde
dentro questo pianto, a giro d'ombra
consunto di deserto, nútre e dopo solca —
il regno di un volto che non guarda
l'opera che sono, mutando in suo rovescio
il lungo mio profilo inciso a fenditura
nel rosso dell'aurora : chi piange —
è questo duro chiasso di orme solo terse
nel luogo senza bosco, è corpo,
corpo che non sente, il vortice di luce
nel vento pronunciato e sempre respirato —
a periplo del Tempo, a terra che consacra
la notte alle sue stelle —

_____

Eighth Station - Jesus Consoles the Women of Jerusalem

A star that roams inside its own portent
molds then cuts through the cedar trees and the stork,
and the heart, the heart of all of you, descended
on slow wings into this weeping, a desert-worn
shadow turning in circles, a star that nourishes then cuts —
through the kingdom of a face that does not look
at the purpose of my existence, but changes to its opposite
my long profile dug as a crevice
into the dawn's red: what cries —
is this harsh din of footfalls only spotless
in a place that knows no woods, it is the body,
a body that does not feel the vortex of light
always breathed and pronounced in the wind —
into rotating Time, into an earth that consecrates
the night to its stars —

———————————

Nona Stazione - Gesù cade per la terza volta

Sopito è forse l'amore intorno
che di nuovo è nuovo ricadere, a farsi carità,
essenza verticale nata in visi immensi,
ebbra sola voce mossa dal suono di se stessa,
da reggersi col soffio, incessante e a nuovo palmo,
dell'ultimo mio sguardo? Gli occhi, solo gli occhi,
fusi con le rocce plasmano di stella il punto in cui si apre
un monte in lontananza, in cui mondi —
scintillano di notte a sorgente di pura frasca,
a turbine di moti, risorti, a vortice sull'acqua —
nel bagliore dell'unica Parola che immobile si spande
serbando ripetutamente l'ora e sempre —
vissuto a prima volta, il passo tuo di veglia
venuta a sabbia di cicala —

_____

Ninth Station - Jesus Falls the Third Time

Has the love around me, perhaps, dozed off
so that it is new again to fall anew, to become charity,
the vertical essence born of immense faces,
intoxicated essence, the only voice moved by its own sound,
sustained by the breath of my last gaze,
never-ending, a new handspan? The eyes, only the eyes,
fused to the rocks star-mold the point where a mountain
opens up in the distance and worlds —
shine at night as a source of pure branches,
an eddy of motions whirling over water —
reborn into the glow of the only Word that, immobile, unfurls
repeatedly preserving the now and always —
as they were first lived, the step that you are taking
in the wakefulness which nears as cicadas' sand —

———————

DECIMA STAZIONE - GESÙ È SPOGLIATO DELLE VESTI

Io, la rondine di Dio, sprotetta e sfigurata,
venni qui sospinta nel tempo che è comune —
ombra già dismessa, inerme mondo di paura
che disfa a casa vuota il margine pietoso
tra il corpo e questa croce, un' orazione povera a silenzio,
tessuta in doppio filo, come calco, cálco —
di un ventre enigma a dismisura, io —
la rondine di Dio, venni qui sospinta, nuda e sfigurata,
nell'aria diventata orma non di scherno, ma di bocca —
furiosa del suo affanno, di un grido tutto già riposto
sull'uscio appena aperto, dove nascere e morire
è istante denso e nominato, refolo che cresce
sul rivolo di un giorno etérno di farfalle —

———————

Tenth Station - Jesus Is Stripped of His Garments

I, God's swallow, unprotected and disfigured,
was driven here in a time that is but common —
cast-off shadow, a helpless world of fear
that undoes into an empty house the pious margin
between the body and this cross, a poor, silent prayer,
woven in double thread, as a cast, the cast —
of a womb that is an incommensurate enigma, I —
God's swallow, was driven here, naked and disfigured,
in the air turned footprint not of scorn, but of a mouth —
furious in its worry, of a scream already laid
at the recently opened door, where to be born and to die
is an instant dense and named, a gust expanding
over the brook of an eternal day of butterflies —

———————————

Undicesima stazione - Gesù è inchiodato in croce

Vada questa notte dritta dentro casa,
passando per il viale a mura che si abbassa
sfondandosi negli occhi, un viale, un viale senza luce
dove la voce che si sente è sull'orlo —
dell'orrido più puro, flebile sul corpo
sfatto e ricomposto in ordine di croce. Vada —
dove saliranno tra gli alberi leggeri, bianchi di cicogna,
tutte le buone terre, le palpebre dischiuse, a scalzo —
moto della luce. E sia, a casa, il Tempo che ripete
l'estremo attimo che tocca l'albero a bisogno
di un tronco più leggero, e il tutto —
e il mare e il mondo a chiodo trapassati,
forzando, inauditi voli di discesa, fragori —
di semplici e ritorti nomi sigillati tersi —
alla finestra —

_____

ELEVENTH STATION - JESUS IS NAILED TO THE CROSS

Let this night go straight and quickly home,
passing through the walled boulevard that dips
as it bursts into the eyes, a boulevard, a lightless boulevard
where the voice that is heard is on the edge —
of the purest horror, feeble on the body
undone and recomposed in the shape of the cross. Let it go —
where all the fair lands will rise through the slight,
stork-white trees, eyelids open, like the light's —
barefoot motion. And let Time be at home, repeating
the ultimate moment that touches the tree craving
a slighter trunk, touches the all —
and the nail-pierced sea and world,
forcing unheard-of downward flights, clamors —
of simple and contorted names sealed pristine —
in the window —

———————————

DODICESIMA STAZIONE - GESÙ MUORE IN CROCE

Davvero sono uomo
che muore sulla croce, o l'assenza
del tempo dal mio viso
è lume di salvezza, tacita speranza
del Sempre che risuona? Il corpo, Madre,
non ha spessore, ma forza
per essere quel volo lì oltre la penombra,
memoria che si sposta —
dal mondo della forma. E il peso,
quello in cui io sono,
è quanto mi sorprende, e la morte
è il rumore che si sente
sovrapponendo materia e essenza,
limitando lo spazio sulla soglia,
arrancando dove nell'ebbrezza
è sbalzo di terra sopra l'acqua
l'ombra suscitata da infrante
essenze di parola. E il tuo sguardo,
Madre, è l'arco che mi tiene, più forte
di un gesto mio di presenza,
vertice tenace di ogni lunga veglia
qui vera a trasparenza —
nel nostro nudo incontro
di amore - e ore —

———————

Twelfth Station - Jesus Dies on the Cross

Am I truly a man
who dies on the cross, or is time's
absence from my face
the light of salvation, tacit hope
of the echoing Always? The body, Mother,
has no depth, but strength
in order to be that flight beyond the half-light,
memory moving away —
from the world of form. And weight,
in which I now dwell,
is what surprises me, and death
is the noise that we hear
when matter and essence *are superimposed*,
limiting the space on the threshold,
plodding on where in the exhilaration
the shadow raised from the essences
of broken words becomes a ledge
of land on water. And your gaze,
Mother, is the arch that holds me, stronger
than my gesture of presence,
tenacious vertex of a long vigil
true, here, because made in the transparence —
of our naked encounter
of hours and love —

Tredicesima Stazione - Gesù è deposto dalla croce

Pura fronda già piena di sua luce
ridiscende ora la ferita e poggia, silenziosa,
anime di forme a molli ondulazioni
nel grembo di questa sola terra, a slancio,
riflessa nelle nubi : squarcio, identico nel grido,
di ali e di capanno, nodo del Sempre che dirama
sillabe di nomi e punti e moti
di túmidi respiri : échi amati e trasmutati
in perfetti cerchi costruiti
nell'annullo di ombra e di distanza, percorsi
fino al vero cielo, divenuto suolo —
a peso di bagliore, materia di píccola boscaglia
pensata di Parola, a cuore di allodola che pulsa
sciogliendo in nuove stelle fisse l'albero da aprire
a spasmo della luce —

Thirteenth Station - Jesus Is Taken Down from the Cross

As pure frond already filled with its light
the wound comes off the cross and quietly
lays souls shaped like soft undulations
into the womb of this one earth that leaps up
to reflect itself in the clouds : a gash of wings and hut
similar in their scream, tangle of the Always spreading
syllables of names and points and motions
of tumid breaths : echoes beloved and transformed
into perfect circles built in the erasure of shadow
and distance, traveled up to the true heaven
which under light's weight turns into ground —
into a matter of underbrush conceived as divine Word,
throbbing as a lark's heart when it melts
the tree that must be opened in light's spasm
into new fixed stars —

———————————

Quattordicesima Stazione - Gesù deposto nel sepolcro

Eterea condensa questa sosta
l'allodola a radice alta di germoglio,
le braccia ampliate di se stesse dove quiete
è il lampo dell'inverno, il mondo —
sull'orlo ripiegato di un unico giardino : *la luce,*
perpetua dello sguardo, nel suo lungo enumerare,
numerare a punto fermo, il tempo che si avvera —
la mínima sequenza di case tutte andate
in cima, in cima alla collina, dove, il labbro,
in forma di prodigio, intese tutto il balbettio
in vibrante semplice discorso, in sazie —
voci da ridire, decifrando i lunghi e articolati
diaframmi, diagrammi, delle foglie —

———————

Fourteenth Station - Jesus Is Laid in the Tomb

Ethereally this station condenses
the tall-sprouted skylark,
the arms that extend where quiet
is winter's lightning, the world—
folding in upon the edge of one garden: the gaze's
perpetual *light*, in its long reckoning,
its orderly reckoning of time coming true—
the smallest sequence of houses all gone
up the hill, to the hilltop, where the portent-shaped lip
weaves all babbling into simple
vibrant speech, into sated—
voices to be relayed, deciphering the leaves'
long, articulated diaphragms, diagrams—

———————————

Quindicesima Stazione - Gesù è risorto

E puro sulla brina venne a costruirsi
un suono già perpetuo, di chiaro non sapersi
la notte che mi hai scritto : *un tetto* —
diafano e leggero, a volto già curvato
fino all'orizzonte, *al lembo* ultimo del cielo : a-
natra che alza, in volo sopra l'acqua,
estreme lingue di covoni, pércettibili a bagliori
continui e silenziosi, echi, mossi trasparenti,
nell'eterna ondulazione di aurore a Sempre cadenzate
su un campo che increspa infine a lepre —
aspersa e *lú-ccicante* —

———————————

Fifteenth Station - Jesus Rises from the Dead

And a pure sound came to build itself
on the frost, a sound perpetual, luminously unknowing
of the night you had written for me: *a roof* —
diaphanous and light, a face already curving
to touch the horizon, the outermost *hem* of the sky:
a *duck* kicking up, as it flies over water,
the outer tongues off sheaves, perceptible in the quiet,
continuous flares, transparent echoes in the eternal
undulation of dawns in lockstep with the Always
over a field that at last ripples into a hare —
sprinkled and *bright* —

———————————

For a Critical Revisitation of the Via Crucis

Introduction

Undoubtedly, the innocent man who dies on the cross has changed the history of humanity. It has changed it both historically, causing a break in Time (before and after Christ), and ethically, with that revolutionary and so often unheeded message, a message that cannot ever stop sounding unreasonable, even paradoxical: "Love thy neighbor as thyself".

This epochal and ethical upheaval cannot be reduced to a purely religious question. This is not about accepting or denying a particular faith. Rather, it is about confronting an event, a narrative which cannot leave us indifferent. And precisely because it cannot leave us indifferent, it never stops being relevant to us in the present time.

The Via Crucis, also known as Via Dolorosa, recounts an event that occurred between 30 and 36 AD in a Jerusalem laboring under Roman rule, on whose veracity almost all historians concur: the sentencing to death and crucifixion of a man called Jesus, also known as Christ.

The most thorough retelling of this event is contained in the gospels, the evangelical documents that recount the life of Jesus. As is well-known, many versions of the gospels exist. The Catholic Church acknowledges as canonical only the gospels attributed to Matthew, Mark, Luke and John, deeming apocryphal (though not completely unfounded or inauthentic) the dozens of other accounts of Jesus's life that have spread since the II century AD.

It wasn't until well into the Middle Ages (around 1150 AD) that the cult of the Via Crucis began to evolve from a simple piece of oral storytelling into a more complex devotional narrative structured around the Passion of Jesus, whose current form, articulated in fourteen "Stations of the Cross", has been attested in Spain since the early XVII century.

The sequence of fourteen Stations is represented in the interior of all Catholic churches, usually in the form of paintings, bas-reliefs, panels, or symbolic crosses.

Besides the traditional Via Crucis, the Catholic Church allows for different versions, provided they are not at variance with the gospels. The most well-known is the so-called "scriptural" Via Crucis, in which the Stations not specifically referred to in the scriptures—such as Jesus's three falls (III, V, VII), Jesus's encounter with his Mother (IV) and with Veronica (VI)—are missing, while other Stations appear in their stead: Jesus praying at Gethsemane (I), Judas's betrayal (II), Peter's denial of Jesus (IV), Pilate's judgment (V), Jesus's promise to the Good Thief (XI), Jesus speaking to his Mother and Beloved Disciple (XII).

The two main versions of the Via Crucis, then, unfold as follows:

Station	Traditional Via Crucis	Scriptural Via Crucis
I	Jesus is condemned to death	Jesus prays at Gethsemane
II	Jesus accepts the cross	Jesus, betrayed by Judas, is arrested
III	Jesus falls for the first time	Jesus is condemned by the Sanhedrin
IV	Jesus meets his sorrowing mother	Jesus is denied by Peter
V	Simon of Cyrene carries the cross of Jesus	Jesus is judged by Pilate
VI	Veronica wipes the face of Jesus	Jesus is scourged and crowned with thorns
VII	Jesus falls a second time	Jesus carries the cross
VIII	Jesus meets the women of Jerusalem	Simon of Cyrene carries the cross of Jesus
IX	Jesus falls a third time	Jesus meets the women of Jerusalem
X	Jesus is stripped of his clothes	Jesus is crucified
XI	Jesus is nailed to the cross	Jesus promises paradise to the Good Thief
XII	Jesus dies on the cross	Jesus speaks to his Mother and the Beloved Disciple
XIII	Jesus is taken down from the cross	Jesus dies on the cross
XIV	Jesus is laid in the tomb	Jesus is laid in the tomb

The Via Crucis today

In modern, secularized societies the Via Crucis, while perceived by the nonbeliever as a centuries-old devotional practice, still incites a profound respect for the figure of Jesus Christ and his earthly hardships. The story of an innocent man sold out and condemned to death on the cross could hardly fail to. On the other hand, it is true that in the last two millennia there have been many victims of similar injustice. And it might be argued that, in a society dominated by notions of power, prestige and rugged individualism, a man who let himself be executed out of love of his neighbor can easily be seen as the ultimate "loser". From this perspective, then, the Via Crucis can be perceived as a somewhat unattractive, even anachronistic, narrative.

However, a more thorough reading of such a narrative uncovers themes that have been relevant throughout history and that remain extraordinarily current.

The ideological theme

The Via Crucis narrates the execution of a man whose words and acts forced his interlocutors to do something completely destabilizing: to look within themselves and unmask, with unheard-of determination, all previously adhered-to falsehoods, hypocrisy and moral ambiguities. By embracing the poor and the outcast, and chasing the merchants from the temple, Jesus subverted the received values of his times. Through his outrageous words and acts, he called upon his listeners to lay bare their conscience by stripping it of its self-serving defenses and rationalizations.

Something similar had already happened, a few centuries before, with Socrates, who had been condemned to drink hemlock for corrupting the Athenian youth—that is, for educating them to self-knowledge, and introducing them to virtue and the Good, new ethical principles that ran counter to state laws and religion. But while Socrates's astute teachings may have shaken up the realm of philosophical speculation, Jesus's words, in their shocking simplicity, have impacted absolutely everyone.

Because he stirred everyone's conscience, Jesus was deemed a dangerous political agitator, a man who destabilizes the law by undermining the ideology that sustains it, and who for this reason deserves to die. In our times, too, those who speak to people's consciences, who disturb the status quo by denouncing the established order, are often marginalized, their voices silenced—though in general by less gruesome means. Jesus and the Via Crucis are, then, the first imprint of an unstoppable movement that makes everyone's conscience and its exegetic potential into a powerful tool for social critique. At the same time they emblematize the scandal of condemning a man who has not committed any crime other than daring to speak to people's consciences and making them question ideology.

The social theme
The context in which the Via Crucis unfolds evinces a collective behavior which is eminently repeatable, and which, in fact, has reoccurred countless times in different social milieus throughout history. Let us examine the main actors. There is Pilate, the Roman governor who administers justice and cannot find fault with the man whom the Jewish high priests have delivered to him. At a

loss for any grounds for charging Jesus, Pilate turns to the other actor, the mob gathered before his house. "What wrong has he done?", he asks. The mob does not offer an answer, but shouts: "Crucify him!"

It is at this point that personal interest and group dynamics come into play. Having failed to find fault with Jesus, Pilate should act according to justice and set him free; but if he did, the mob would rise up. On the other hand, by sentencing him to death, the mob would be appeased, the prestige of the Roman Empire would be preserved, and his own position would be strengthened, but then he would have committed an injustice. What to do? Strikingly, Pilate does not choose either course of action, and rather finds what to him might have sounded like the perfect compromise to save both himself and his conscience: he declines to pronounce Jesus guilty, because he knows he is not, and in so doing he acts like a fair judge. But since he is also a governor tasked with maintaining order, he chooses to stave off an uprising by allowing the mob to decide Christ's fate.

As for the exulting mob, it is no other than a group of individuals who, in the anonymity of the crowd, have shed their rationality to embrace the behavior of crazed animals. The crowd yelling "Crucify him!" exhibits what today we would define "mob behavior", that is, the identification of each of its members into a super-individual constituted by the virtual sum of all individuals, whereby logical normality is abandoned in the name of a collective instinct.

In this respect, a sociopsychological reading of the Via Crucis offers penetrating (and still very relevant) truths about how people in a crowd may easily lose their psychic and moral equilibrium and yield to irrational fear and a violent response.

The political theme

The Via Crucis is also a dispassionate treatise on politics. Besides Pilate, the embodiment of political calculation, other political characters populate this chronicle of a death foretold. Chief among them are the high priests of the Sanhedrin, whose job it is to guarantee that even under Roman rule, Jewish laws will continue to be applied without exception. They are the ones who capture Jesus and determine that he is guilty of crimes punishable by death. Yet, their hands will not be stained with his blood. Because they lack the power to materially carry out a death sentence, they must turn Jesus over to the Roman authorities with their recommendation. Roman governor Pilate, who cannot bring himself to find Christ guilty, will in turn deliver him over to the mob.

It is the perfect representation of a ruthless political game whose players share power and administer it in a cynical, calculating way, all the while refusing to take responsibility for the bloodshed they cause.

The psychological theme

Like a mirror held up to our psyche, the Stations of the Via Crucis contain a rich taxonomy of archetypal human situations. Here is a short list:

Being unfairly judged or punished
Being betrayed by a friend
Having to carry the weight of the world on one's shoulders
Having (repeatedly) to pick oneself up after a fall.
Receiving the comfort of close friends

Receiving unexpected help from a stranger
Enduring physical pain
Feeling helpless, stripped of all dignity
Feeling alone in the world

The psychological fabric of the Via Crucis is complex, an inexhaustible mosaic that enjoins us to reflect on our human vulnerabilities. The narrative is set in motion by two mirroring betrayals: Judas's and Peter's, the former driven by greed, the latter by cowardice. They both will eventually atone for their weaknesses, Judas by experiencing remorse and Peter by repenting. Human vulnerabilities shine through in all the characters of the Via Crucis, who at some point or other experience sentiments ranging from grief to solace, from despair to hope, from defeat to love. Through the staging of these feelings, the narrative of the Via Crucis establishes an intimate rapport with readers called to identify themselves with the foibles and virtues of its actors.

In the course of our lives, each of us is likely to experience injustice, betrayal, hypocrisy and falsehood. Sometimes we are on the receiving end of such offenses, sometimes we are the ones inflicting them on others. But we are also capable of being the bestowers, as well as the recipients, of generosity, loyalty, justice, and love. Constant oscillation between high and low is a characteristic of our human condition; the Way of the Cross offers a potent compendium that speaks to readers in all times and places. It is no other than the narrative of ourselves, the chronicle of our difficult path through life.

The Via Crucis of the downtrodden

The actors in the Via Crucis are legion, an exceptionally lucid tapestry of human life. We have already discussed those characters who, thanks to the power vested in them, play an active role in Christ's fate: Pilate, the Sanhedrin, the mob. Next to them, however, are a host of characters whom we could define as "humble" or "poor", in that, having no power, they are forced to endure each painful event.

Chief among them is Mary, the Mother of Jesus, who silently accompanies her son on his calvary. Through her deafening silence, though, Mary embodies the quiet strength of all mothers in the face of utmost grief. She has embraced her grief with unflagging determination, has made it part of her entire existence and will bear witness to it for all humankind. It is no wonder that, almost two thousand years later, Russian poet Anna Akhmatova (1889-1966) will think of Mary as she laments—in *Requiem*—the fate of her son imprisoned by the Stalinist regime, knowing that only through Mary will she be able to give her pain some shape and deal with it.

Next to Mary we have John, the Beloved Disciple: as they both suffer through the moment in which they are stripped of everything worth living, they are united by the shared love for the man on the cross. Though love cannot vanquish death, it creates the strongest possible bond between the two mourners, and between each of them and the memory of the deceased, so that death will not prevail over remembrance. The fact that Jesus entrusts Mary and John to each other reveals that human closeness is the only solace we have against death. Even in our times, closeness in the face of death is often a transformative moment that has the potential to free us from the egoism and loneliness that characterize our society.

Among the humble characters we may certainly include Simon of Cyrene, who helps Jesus carry the cross, the women of Jerusalem, the Roman guards who draw lots for Christ's garments at the foot of the cross, the centurion who thrusts the spear into Christ's side, and Dismas, the Good Thief. It is perhaps this very collection of the downtrodden that embodies most effectively the universality of the human condition, evincing a range of traits and behaviors that we are forced to recognize as inherently our own.

The Via Crucis of the absent

There are also characters that, while absent from the narrative, still leave their imprint on it.

The first is Herod Antipas, tetrarch of Galilee. Before washing his hands of Jesus, Pilate asks Herod to deal with him. Unable to find fault with the prisoner, Herod sends him back to Pilate. According to Luke, the episode even causes the two officials to develop a friendship, as they are brought together by their common cynicism in the shadow of the Cross.

The second absent actor, surprisingly, is Jesus's disciples. The loyal companions who have stuck with Jesus day in day out, who, upon being summoned by him, have given up everything to follow him—as the tragedy unfolds, they are nowhere to be seen. What might have happened to that small group of fanatics who seemed ready to die for him and instead flee as soon as the soldiers come for their Teacher? It is not difficult to imagine their best intentions being hampered by fear and cowardice, feelings we all relate to and which are a constant throughout history.

Lastly, we have the people who witness in silence as Jesus suffers through his calvary, common people who might have seen a new light in that revolutionary who has walked their streets. Three days later, in Luke's narrative, we encounter two of them on the road to Emmeus, two disciples intent on discussing the passion and death of Christ. Many more will be found throughout history, all the way down to our times. Each of us, too, belongs in their ranks, as to this day we ourselves haven't made complete sense of the Christ-event, not knowing how to behave in the face of the scandal embodied by the Man on the Cross, a just man who was executed for preaching justice and love for our neighbor, including for those who would abandon, scorn, and betray him.

In conclusion

The more we delve into the Via Crucis, the more we analyze the tapestry of human situations and demeanors that animate it, the more we realize that the religious sphere to which it is usually confined is insufficient and constraining. The narrative's unflinching exploration of the ethical, ideological, social, political, and psychological aspects of Christ's calvary is what elevates it into a universal story that addresses everyone independently of their creed. The extraordinary concentration of pain, injustice, love and humility contained in the Via Crucis's few tableaux has made it possible for its message to last through the centuries without losing any of its relevance, undiminished by the vagaries of cultural fashion and historical change.

All that has occurred in any historical time was already contained or foreshadowed in the Via Crucis. History repeats and will continue to repeat itself, as humans of all generations continue to fall into predictable behavioral patterns evincing the very same virtues and flaws.

The Way of the Cross tells the story of what we were, what we are, and what we will be. To read it and reread it, to ponder it, and to become inspired anew by it means to be able to recognize in it the mystery of our existence on this earth, the way we navigate our existential journey as best we can under the weight of our own crosses.

Through the turbulence of our lives, the Man on the Cross remains firmly on the horizon like a star shedding its hopeful light on humanity, time, and history.

Acknowledgments

I would like to extend my warmest thanks to Marc Estrin, who looked in depth into the lyrics of *Via Crucis* and showed me the most efficient way to organize them for this English-language edition.

A big thank you also to Donna Bister for the stellar quality of the book's design as well as for the beautiful cover.

A special thank you goes to Giorgio Mobili, whose care and love for these poems shine through in his luminous English translation.

Lastly, I am grateful to Roberto Uberti for his invaluable insight in the redaction of the essay that accompanies this collection.

About the Author

Born near Turin, Italy, in 1969, Silvia Comoglio is an Italian poet whose writing is tightly bound up with the home in which she has lived since birth, and which has belonged to her family since the 1800s. This home is a quaint water mill whose main construction dates back as far as the 1300s. Because of the water still flowing under the foundations, eventually becoming a waterfall, everything in the house is always clattering and whispering. But its centuries-old stones are not just stones: they are the custodians of past ages that have witnessed the toil and pain, as well as the love and solidarity, of entire generations. (During World War II, the mill was a haven for scores of refugees and a hiding place for the Italian *partigiani*.) Nor is the water one hears babbling day and night just water: rather, it is the very sound and rhythm of time, the road to understanding Time. Water is also the source of Silvia's phonosymbolic research, of her interest in parsing and juxtaposing sounds in an attempt to illuminate their relationship to sense—a constant preoccupation in her work. The stones as custodians of History, and water as the embodiment of Time, thus, provide the coordinates for Silvia Comoglio's explorations, both in the field of poetry and philosophy (in which she majored). Though her writing may at times appear abstract or visionary, it is in fact firmly grounded in a present that bears the indelible traces of our historical past. There is no eluding Time and History: we move on a stage defined by the complexities of their interaction and the stubbornness of their recurrence.

About the Translator

A poet, translator, critic, and photographer, Giorgio Mobili was born in Milan, Italy, in 1973. He teaches at California State University, Fresno. He is the author of several academic essays on (Post)modern literature and film, and of the book *Irritable Bodies and Postmodern Subjects in Pynchon, Puig, and Volponi* (2008).

His Italian poetry has appeared in several journals and in six published collections, and has been anthologized in *Poets of the Italian Diaspora*. A Spanish-language collection (*Última salida a Ventura*) came out in Santiago, Chile, in 2014. His poetry has been translated into English, Spanish, and Romanian. In 2021 came his first English-language book of poetry and photography, *Sunken Boulevards*. In 2024 he co-authored *La casa gialla*, a collaboration where Mobili's photographies engage in a haunting dialogue with Silvia Comoglio's verse.

As a translator he has rendered into Italian the poets Narlan Matos, Christopher Merrill, Carmen Berenguer, and Malú Urriola. He has translated into English poets Luigi Fontanella, Alessio Brandolini and Silvia Comoglio, and philosopher Massimo Cacciari.

Fomite

Writing a review on social media sites for readers will help the progress of independent publishing. To submit a review, go to the book page on any of the sites and follow the links for reviews. Books from independent presses rely on reader-to-reader communications.

For more information or to order any of our books, visit:
http://www.fomitepress.com/our-books.html

More dual language titles from Fomite

Vito Bonito/Alison Grimaldi Donahue — Soffiata Via/Blown Away

Antonello Borra/Blossom Kirschenbaum — Alfabestiario

Antonello Borra/Blossom Kirschenbaum — AlphaBetaBestiaro

Antonello Borra/Anis Memon — Fabbrica delle idee/The Factory of Ideas

Alessio Brandolini/Giorgio Mobili — Miniature Cities

Jeannette Clariond/Lawrence Schimel — Desert Memory

Lorenzo Carlucci/Todd Portnowitz — Methods

Tina Escaja/Mark Eisner — Caída Libre/Free Fall

Luigi Fontanella/Giorgio Mobili — L'Adolescenza e la notte/Adolescence and Night

Hösle, Johannes/Marc Estrin — Album aus Dietenbronn/Whatever Befalls

Aristea Papalexandrou/Philip Ramp —Μας προσπερνά/It's Overtaking Us

Katerina Anghelaki-Rooke//Philip Ramp — Losing Appetite for Existence

Mikis Theodoraksi/Gail Holst-Warhaft — The House with the Scorpions

Paolo Valesio/Todd Portnowitz — La Mezzanotte di Spoleto/Midnight in Spoleto

More poetry from Fomite...

Anna Blackmer — Hexagrams

L. Brown — Loopholes

Sue D. Burton — Little Steel

Christine Butterworth-McDermott — Evelyn As

Christine Butterworth-McDermott — The Spellbook of Fruit and Flowers

David Cavanagh— Cycling in Plato's Cave

Fomite

Fomite